My First Communion Journal

This journal belongs to:

It was given to me by:

On this date:

Jesus said to them,
"I am the bread of life;
whoever comes to me will
never hunger, and whoever
believes in me will never
thirst." – John 6:35

***Nihil obstat*:**
Rev. Timothy Hall,
Censor librorum
April 11, 2018

***Imprimatur*:**
†Most Rev. John M. Quinn,
Bishop of Winona
April 11, 2018

Cover and interior design and composition by Laurie Nelson, Agápe Design Studios.

Copy editing by Karen Carter.

The cover illustration and the interior illustrations of the child saints and the Eucharist on pages 3, 20, 24, 28, 30, 32, and 38 are by Jen Norton. www.jennortonartstudio.com

24 23 22 21 20 19 2 3 4 5 6 7 8 9

ISBN: 978-1-68192-503-5 (Inventory No. T2392)
LCCN: 2019939972

Our Sunday Visitor, Inc., 200 Noll Plaza, Huntington, IN 46750; 1-800-348-2440; www.osv.com

Acknowledgments

The statement by Pope Francis on page 5 is from "Pope Francis Recalls His 1st Communion, Says to Remember Catechists," published on December 15, 2014, by ZENIT news service.

The statement by Pope Benedict XVI on page 34 is from "Catechetical Meeting of the Holy Father with Children Who Had Received Their First Communion During the Year," October 15, 2005, St. Peter's Square. Accessed at vatican.va.

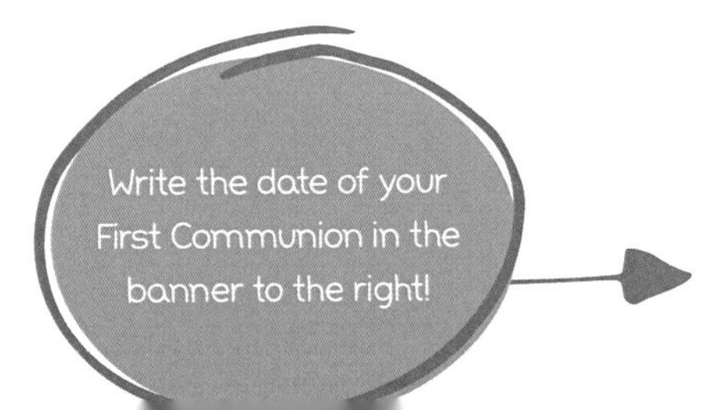

DO THIS TO
REMEMBE
the NEW COVENANT of MY BLOOD Shed for you
welcome
friend
THIS is MY Body TO BE given up for You
JNORTON

"You, who will make your First Communion,
always remember that day your whole life:
the first day that Jesus came into us.
He comes, makes himself one with us,
makes himself our food,
our nourishment to give us strength."

–Pope Francis

An ICON of ME

An *icon* is a simple painting of a holy person. It uses symbols such as clothes, colors, and objects to show how the person is special to God. On another piece of paper, draw an "icon" of you. Include symbols that show who you are. Then tape it here.

My name is ______________________________.

I was given this name because ______________________________
______________________________.

These are the people in my family: ______________________________
____
____

I was born on ______________ and baptized on ______________.

in the parish of ______________________________.

I go to school at ______________________________.

Some of my friends are: ______________________________
____
______________________________.

These are some of the talents and gifts God has given me:
____
____
____
____

These are my favorites:
____
____
____

YOU ARE A BELOVED CHILD OF GOD

Did you know that when you were baptized, you were **"born again"** into a spiritual family? It's true!

When Jesus was baptized, the Holy Spirit descended on him, and God the Father said, "You are my beloved Son; with you I am well pleased" (Luke 3:22).

When you were baptized, the Holy Spirit came down on you and gave you a new life, and made you a child of God...his beloved daughter or son.

All the other people who have been born again through the waters of baptism are children of God, too...and in a special way, your brothers and sisters.

After Jesus was baptized, he began his mission. He healed people, and forgave their sins, and showed them God's love.

When you were baptized, you were called to share in Jesus' mission. That's a pretty big responsibility!

The Eucharist is a special food that will give you strength for this mission. The Eucharist is the body and blood of Jesus. Through the Eucharist, Jesus comes into you. He brings you closer to God the Father, and helps you complete your part of his mission to bring God's love to the whole world.

So, as you get older, if you ever wonder who you are, remember: before anything else, you are a child of God...and God has given you a mission that only you can do!

"Before I formed you in the womb
I knew you, and before you were born
I consecrated you ...."

—Jeremiah 1:5

God said these words to Jeremiah when he was very young. God says these words to you, too! God knew who you were before you were born. Even then, God consecrated you. To be ***consecrated*** means to be set aside for a special, holy purpose. What special purpose do you think God has planned for you?

BAPTISM MEMORIES

Ask your parents or godparents to share the story of the day you were born, and the day you were baptized. You can write the story here, or ask them to write it for you.

WHAT IF JESUS CAME TO YOUR HOUSE?

Jesus liked to eat meals with all sorts of people. Do you remember when he told Zacchaeus that he was coming to his house for dinner? How about the time Jesus multiplied the loaves and fishes for thousands of hungry people? He ate meals at the houses of important religious leaders, and he ate meals at the houses of people no one else liked. And he shared a special meal, the Last Supper, with his closest friends on the night before he died.

It's no wonder Jesus chose bread and wine as a way of sharing himself with us always!

Imagine Jesus came to your house for dinner. What food would you want to serve him? How would you celebrate?

Jesus looked up
and said to him,
Zacchaeus, come down quickly,
for today I must stay at your house.
And he came down quickly
and received him with joy.

– Luke 19:5–6

BREAD FOR JESUS

Bread was one of the main foods that people ate in Jesus' time. Sometimes, God gave his people special bread to remind them of his care for them. After God freed his people from slavery in Egypt, he gave them a special bread called **manna** so they would not get hungry in the desert. Later, the people placed bread in the presence of God in the Temple.

Once, Jesus asked his disciples to feed a crowd of thousands of people. But where could they get enough food?

A child who had five loaves of bread and two fish shared his food with Jesus. Jesus took the food and gave thanks to God for it. Then the disciples gave it to the people. When everyone was done eating, there were twelve baskets of leftovers! ***(Read the whole story in John 6:1–14.)***

If you would like to make bread for Jesus, try this recipe for ***Unleavened Bread***. This is the same kind of bread the Jewish people made for their journey out of slavery.

Ingredients

1 cup flour

1/3 cup vegetable oil

1/8 teaspoon salt

1/3 cup water

Directions

Preheat the oven to 425°F. Put parchment paper on a baking sheet. Mix the flour, oil, and salt together in a bowl. Add the water and mix using a fork. When the dough is soft, make 6 balls. Press the balls into flat disks. They will look like big cookies. Bake in the oven for 8–10 minutes. Cool before eating.

Ask your parents, grandparents, or godparents to share their favorite bread recipe with you. (Maybe you could even make it together!) Write the recipe down here.

RECIPE: FROM:

INGREDIENTS:

DIRECTIONS:

Jesus said to them, "I am the bread of life; whoever comes to me will never hunger, and whoever believes in me will never thirst." – John 6:35

Did you know the word ***eucharist*** means "thanksgiving"? That is because during the Mass, we give thanks to God for the many gifts he has given us–especially the gift of Jesus! (See how many times you hear the word "thanks" during the Mass.)

What are you thankful for? Write down your "thankful list," and the next time you go to Mass, remember to give thanks!

Let us

GIVE THANKS

TO THE LORD

our God!

—Preface to the Eucharistic Prayer

At every celebration of the Eucharist, we bring gifts to the altar. Bread and wine are brought to the altar. We offer these gifts to God so that they may be changed into spiritual food: the Body and Blood of Jesus Christ.

We bring other gifts, too, including the money that people put in the collection basket. You can bring your own gifts to the altar, too. Besides putting money in the collection, you can give God the spiritual gifts you have prepared throughout the week. You can also give the gift of yourself.

What are your "gifts"? Are you good at sports? Are you funny, or kind, or a talented singer? Write your gifts on the box.

I give you a new commandment: LOVE ONE ANOTHER. AS I HAVE LOVED YOU, SO YOU ALSO SHOULD LOVE ONE ANOTHER.

–John 13:34

During the Last Supper, Jesus washed his friends' dirty feet. He did this to show them that they should serve one another. **"As I have done for you, you should also do," he said** (John 13:15).

Receiving the Eucharist prepares us to serve others in the same way that Jesus did, not just by washing dirty feet, but by being kind and helpful to others, especially those most in need.

Here are some ideas for serving others. Circle the ones you have done, and write in other ways you have served.

ST. THÉRÈSE'S FIRST COMMUNION

Thérèse Martin received her First Communion in Lisieux, France in 1884. She knew that when she received Jesus in the Eucharist, he would come into her heart in a new and special way.

She wanted to make her heart warm and welcoming for Jesus, so she spent the months before her First Communion making many little sacrifices and acts of love. The sacrifice might be something like letting her sister play with her favorite toy, or eating her least-favorite food without complaining. The acts of love could be complimenting her sister, making a gift for a friend, or spending extra time in prayer with Jesus. She also spent time in a quiet corner of her room thinking about God; other times, she included Jesus in the games she played with her sisters.

Thérèse imagined that all of these little sacrifices and acts of love were changed into flowers: violets and roses, cornflowers and daisies, forget-me-nots, and so on. She imagined that these "flowers" were filling her heart to welcome Jesus.

"I wanted all the flowers on the earth to cradle Jesus in my heart," she said.

Many years later, Thérèse remembered her First Communion as one of the most special days of her life. "I knew that I was loved by Jesus, and I said, 'I love you, and I give myself to you forever.'"

SACRIFICES AND ACTS OF LOVE FOR JESUS

Do you want to make little sacrifices and acts of love for Jesus like St. Thérèse did? Write down everything you do here.

DAY	WHAT I DID FOR JESUS

SACRIFICES AND ACTS OF LOVE FOR JESUS

Do you want to make little sacrifices and acts of love for Jesus like St. Thérèse did? Write down everything you do here.

DAY	WHAT I DID FOR JESUS

To receive in truth the Body and Blood of Christ given up for us, we must recognize Christ in the poorest.

–Catechism 1397

Do you realize that Jesus is there in the Eucharist for you alone? He burns with the desire to come into your heart!

–St. Thérèse

Jesus called the children to himself and said, "Let the children come to me and do not prevent them; for the kingdom of God belongs to such as these."

–Luke 18:16

Beloved boys and girls, keep yourselves worthy of Jesus whom you receive! Be innocent and generous! Undertake to make life beautiful for everyone, with obedience, kindness, good manners! The secret of joy is goodness!

–Pope John Paul II, address to First Communicants (1979)

ST. DOMINIC'S FIRST COMMUNION

Dominic Savio loved playing sports and games, and was a good friend to all the other boys at his school.

He made his First Communion in Murialdo, Italy, in the year 1849. Back in those days, children did not receive their First Communion until they were twelve years old. But the parish priest let Dominic receive the Eucharist at the age of seven because he showed such great love of Jesus.

Dominic prepared for his First Communion by reading holy books, praying, and asking his mother's forgiveness for anything he might have done to hurt her. He also kept a little book in which he wrote down prayers and thoughts about God. Before his First Communion, he wrote this in his book:

Resolutions made by me, Dominic Savio, in the year 1849, on the day of my First Communion, at the age of seven.

1. I will go to Confession and Communion as often as possible.
2. I will sanctify Sundays and holy days in a special way.
3. Jesus and Mary will be my friends.
4. Death, but not sin.

Years later, when Dominic talked about his First Communion, he said:

"That was the happiest and most wonderful day of my life."

Resolutions are promises that you make to yourself to do something, and to sanctify something is to make it holy. And Dominic took as his motto the words, "Death, but not sin," to remind himself that it would be better to die and be with God than to sin and be separated from God.

YOUR FIRST COMMUNION RESOLUTIONS

Do you want to make resolutions like St. Dominic Savio did? Write down your own resolutions here.

MY FIRST CONFESSION

Before your First Communion comes your First Confession—the first time you receive the sacrament of Penance and Reconciliation. Tell about your First Confession here: Where was it? Who was there? How did you celebrate afterward?

Keep track of how often you receive the sacrament of Penance and Reconciliation this year. Color one element of this art every time you go to confession. When you're done, you will have a beautiful gift for God... but God loves the gift of yourself even more!

MY CONFESSION RECORD

BLESSED FRANCISCO'S FIRST COMMUNION

How would you like to receive your First Communion from the hands of an angel? That is what happened to Francisco Marto and his sister Jacinta, two children from the country of Portugal, in the autumn of 1916.

At this time a horrible war was happening all across Europe. God wanted everyone to know the war made him very sad. He wanted them to turn away from sin so they could know his love and peace. God chose Francisco and Jacinta and their cousin, Lúcia Santos, to share this message with the world.

The three children often spent long days taking care of their families' sheep. Francisco sometimes played his flute for the girls; other times, he played with little lizards and birds. Francisco and the girls prayed together, too.

One day, an angel appeared to the children. He said he was the Angel of Peace, sent by God to prepare them for their special mission. The angel visited them three times, teaching them how to pray and how to make sacrifices for the love of God.

"Most holy Trinity, I adore you! My God, my God, I love you in the Most Blessed Sacrament!"

On his third visit, the angel brought the body and blood of Jesus Christ in the Eucharist. He taught the children how to pray before the Eucharist, saying: "Most holy Trinity, I adore you! My God, my God, I love you in the Most Blessed Sacrament!"

Then the angel gave the children Holy Communion. Lúcia had already received her First Communion, but Francisco and Jacinta had not. God gave them their first Holy Communion in this way to strengthen them for their important mission.

ADORING JESUS IN THE EUCHARIST

Being close to Jesus in the Eucharist filled Francisco's heart with a beautiful peace, and he went to church as often as he could to pray before Jesus in the tabernacle, the special place where the Eucharist is kept after Mass.

Praying before Jesus in the Eucharist in this way is called *adoration*. Sometimes, people pray with words during adoration, but other times, they are happy just to think about Jesus. It is a quiet sharing of love, like when a child sits in the lap of his or her parent or grandparent.

You can adore Jesus in the Eucharist at your church. Ask your parents or someone who works at your church to show you the tabernacle (or the adoration chapel). Use the space below to write about your time with Jesus.

Day(s) that I adored Jesus in the Eucharist:

What I said to Jesus:

What Jesus said to me:

When you have received Jesus
in the Eucharist,
stir up your heart to praise him;
speak to him about your spiritual life,
gazing upon him in your soul
where he is present for your happiness;
welcome him as warmly as possible,
and behave in such a way that your actions
may give proof to all of his presence.

–St. Francis de Sales

SPEAKING TO JESUS IN YOUR HEART

After receiving the Eucharist, spend time with Jesus in your heart. You might want to imagine sitting with him in your favorite spot.

Write down what you said to Jesus in your heart after your First Communion:

BLESSED LAURA'S FIRST COMMUNION

When the pope declared that Laura Vicuña was blessed, he called her "the Eucharistic flower of Junin de Los Andes," the place where she lived in Argentina.

Laura faced many troubles in her life. Her father died when she was only two, leaving Laura's mother to care for Laura and her sister, Julia, all by herself. Later, the man who lived with Laura's family was very mean to them. He sometimes hit Laura and her mother.

Laura went to a Catholic school. There, the religious sisters taught her about Jesus' presence in the Eucharist. Laura often visited Jesus in the tabernacle, the "little house" where the Eucharist was kept after Mass. Sometimes, she even blew Jesus a kiss!

Like Blessed Dominic, Laura kept a little notebook for writing thoughts and prayers before her First Communion.

"Wherever I am, at school, at play, or anywhere else, the thought of God accompanies me, helps me, and consoles me," she said. And she also wrote this little prayer: "O my God, I want to love you and serve you all my life. I give you my soul, my heart, my whole self."

Laura received her First Communion in 1901, when she was ten years old. During the Mass, she saw that her mother did not receive the Eucharist. She also saw that her mother was very unhappy.

Every day after her First Communion, she visited Jesus in the tabernacle and prayed for her mother: "Jesus, I wish that Mama would know you better and be happy."

Eventually, this prayer was answered when Laura's mother was reunited with Jesus in the Church.

O MY GOD,
I WANT TO LOVE YOU
AND
SERVE YOU ALL MY LIFE.
I GIVE YOU MY SOUL,
MY HEART,
MY WHOLE SELF.

–Blessed Laura Vicuña

POPE BENEDICT'S FIRST COMMUNION

In 2005, Pope Benedict spoke to children who had received their First Communion. They asked him to share the story of his own First Communion. Here is some of what he said:

I remember my First Communion day very well. It was a lovely Sunday in March 1936, 69 years ago. It was a sunny day, the church looked very beautiful, there was music. There were so many beautiful things that I remember. There were about thirty of us, boys and girls from my little village.

But at the heart of my joyful and beautiful memories is this one–and your spokesperson said the same thing: I understood that Jesus had entered my heart, he had actually visited me. And with Jesus, God himself was with me. And I realized that this is a gift of love that is truly worth more than all the other things that life can give.

So on that day I was really filled with great joy, because Jesus came to me and I realized that a new stage in my life was beginning, that it was henceforth important to stay faithful to that encounter, to that communion. I promised the Lord as best I could: "I always want to stay with you," and I prayed to him, "but above all, stay with me." So I went on living my life like that; thanks be to God, the Lord has always taken me by the hand and guided me, even in difficult situations.

Thus, that day of my First Communion was the beginning of a journey made together. I hope that for all of you too, the First Communion you have received will be the beginning of a lifelong friendship with Jesus, the beginning of a journey together, because in walking with Jesus we do well and life becomes good.

I promised the Lord
as best I could:
"I always want to
stay with you,"
and I prayed to him,
"but above all,
stay with me."

MY PATRON SAINT

Do you have a patron saint? A saint is someone who lives with God in heaven, and a patron is someone who takes care of something or someone; so, a patron saint is someone in heaven who is your "spiritual friend," someone who will pray for you and help you to grow in holiness (that is, grow closer to God). Your patron saint should be someone whose way of being holy inspires you, so you can imitate his or her example.

Ask an adult to provide you with a book about the saints so you can read their stories and choose your own patron saint. (You can pray to the Holy Spirit for help!)

Name of my patron saint: ______________________

When my patron saint lived: ______________________

Here is what I like about my patron saint:

____

____

____

____

____

____

____

Write a prayerful letter to your patron saint.

A LETTER TO MY PATRON SAINT

My prayer to Jesus on my First Communion:

MY FIRST COMMUNION DAY

I received my First Communion on

in the parish of .

The presider (person who said Mass) was

.

Clothes I wore:

Friends and family who attended:

Gifts I received:

Food we ate:

The weather was

My favorite part:

MY FIRST COMMUNION DAY

Write down the story of your First Communion Day.

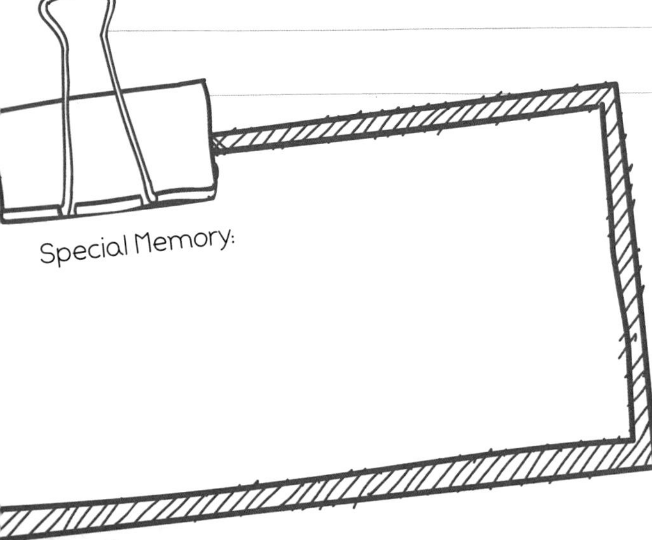

MY FIRST COMMUNION DAY

Do you have pictures from your First Communion Day? Put them here.

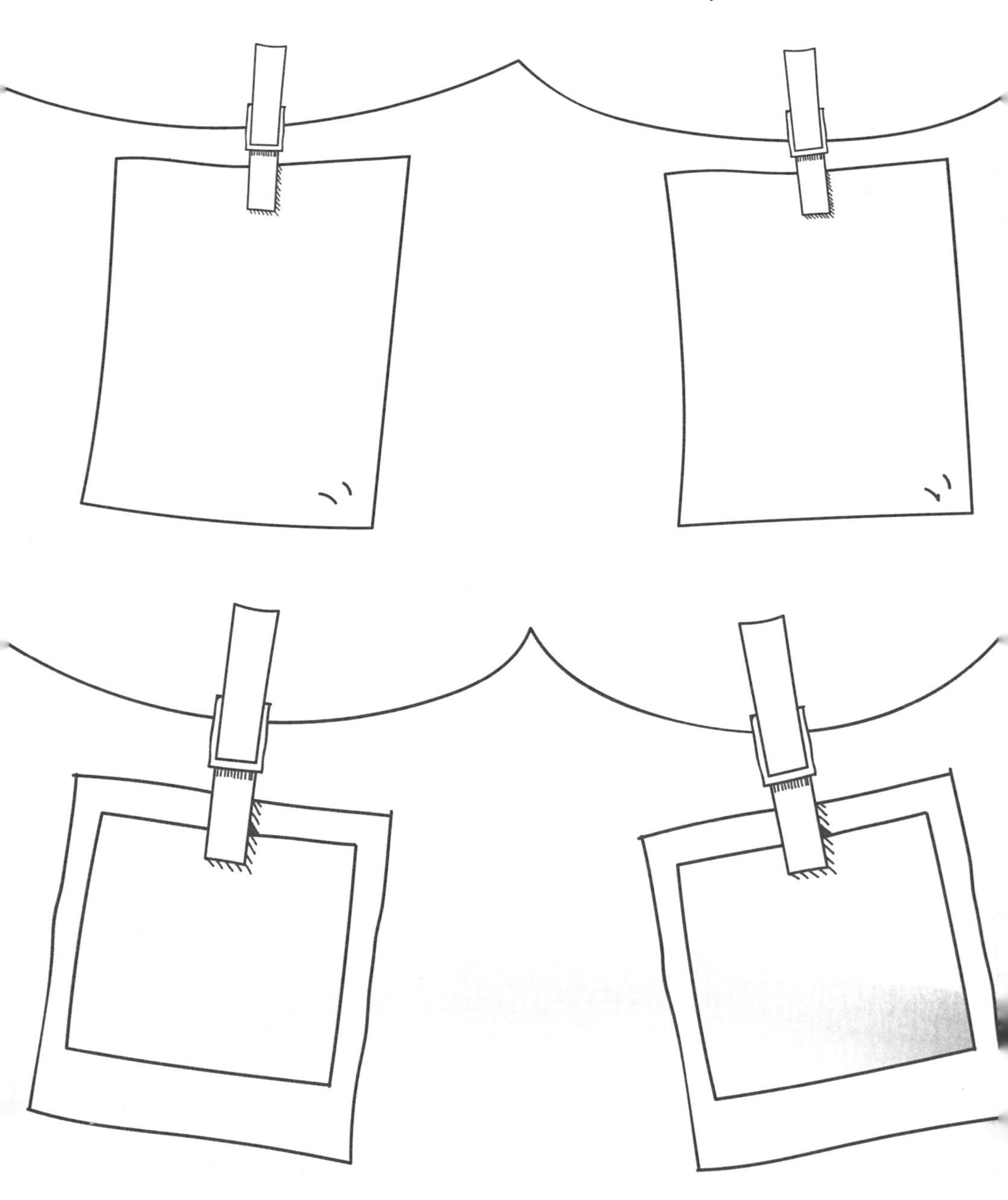

MESSAGES FROM FRIENDS AND FAMILY

Ask friends and family to write a special message to you for your First Communion.

MESSAGES FROM FRIENDS AND FAMILY

MESSAGES FROM FRIENDS AND FAMILY

MESSAGES FROM FRIENDS AND FAMILY

MESSAGES FROM FRIENDS AND FAMILY